D1271785

Rabbi Nosson Scherman / Rabbi Meir Zlotowitz
General Editors

Take Me

Published by

Mesorah Publications, ltd

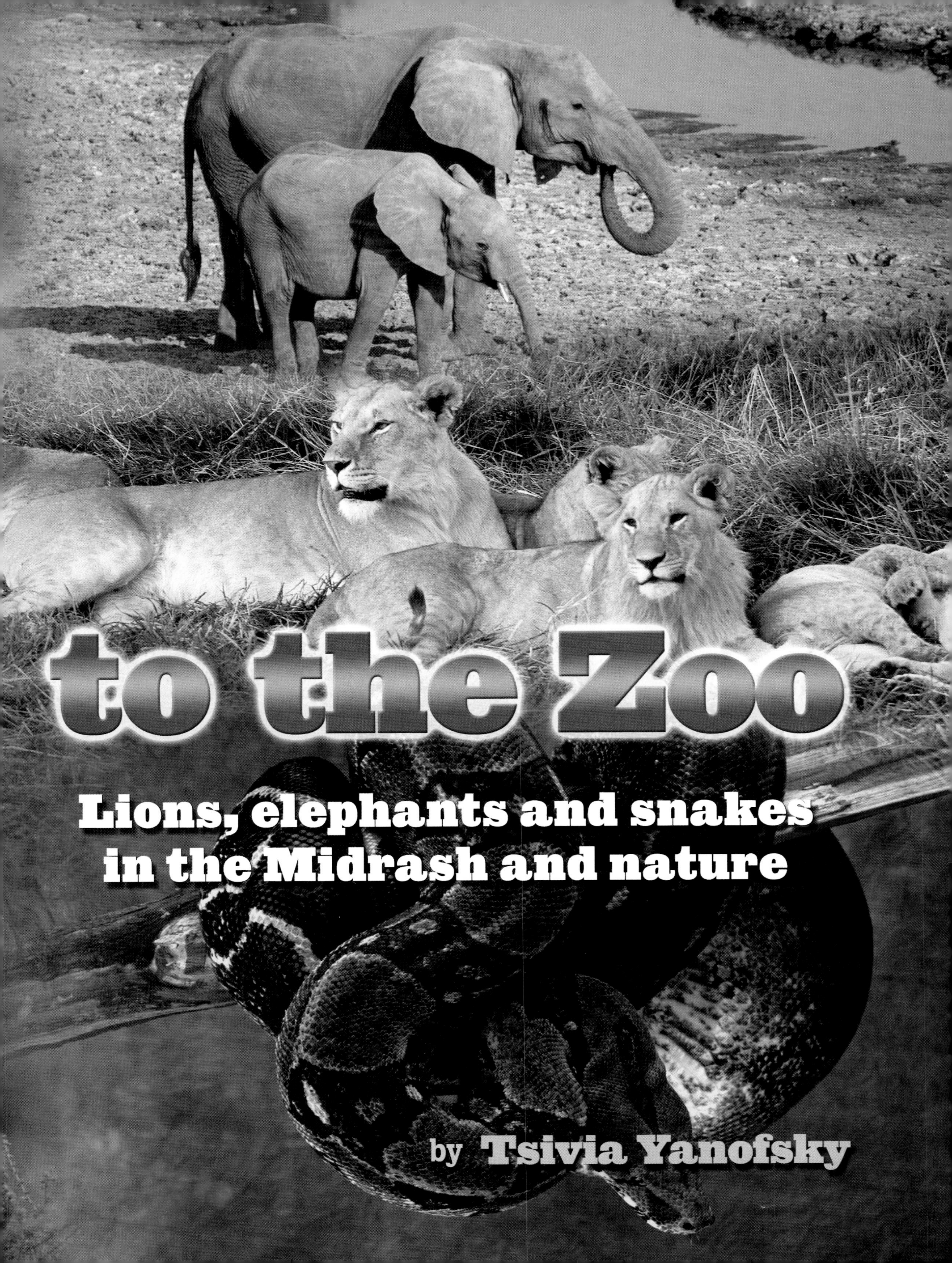
to the Zoo
Lions, elephants and snakes
in the Midrash and nature
by Tsivia Yanofsky

"TAKE ME TO THE ZOO"

First edition – First impression: December, 2003

Published and Distributed by **MESORAH PUBLICATIONS, LTD.**
4401 Second Avenue / Brooklyn, NY 11232 / (718) 921-9000 / Fax: (718) 680-1875 / www.artscroll.com

Distributed in Israel by SIFRIATI / A. GITLER
6 Hayarkon Street / Bnei Brak 51127 / Israel

Distributed in Europe by LEHMANNS
Unit E, Viking Industrial Park / Rolling Mill Road / Jarrow, Tyne & Wear NE32 3DP, England

Distributed in Australia and New Zealand by GOLDS WORLD OF JUDAICA
3-13 William Street / Balaclava Melbourne 3183 / Victoria, Australia

Distributed in South Africa by KOLLEL BOOKSHOP
Shop 8A Norwood Hypermarket / Norwood 2196 / Johannesburg, South Africa

Printed in the United States of America by
Edison Lithographing and Printing Corp. / North Bergen, N.J.
Custom bound by Sefercraft, Inc. / 4401 Second Avenue / Brooklyn N.Y. 11232

ISBN: 1-57819-099-1

Photo Credits

ArtToday: 13, 15 (bottom), 18, 20, 21, 24, 25, 27, 30, 31, 32, 34, 35 (top, center), 39, 40, 41, 49, 54, 59, 60, 61, 62 (bottom), 64, 65, 66, 71, 75, 76, 77, 79 (bottom), 83, 89, 90, 91, 92
Breck P. Kent / Animals Animals: 73
Corel: 16 (bottom), 33, 35 (bottom), 38, 46, 57, 63, 67
Eric Vitiello / ISP: 55
Eyewire: 26, 43, 44, 47, 48, 52-53
Frans Lanting / Minden Pictures: 51, 58
Jaleen Grove, ISP: 94
Joel Satore / National Geographic: 80-81
Kian Khoon Tan / ISP: 87
Konrad Wothe / Minden Pictures: 56
Lukasz Chyrek / ISP: 69
Matt Matthews / ISP: 70
Michael and Patricia Fogden / Minden Pictures: 82, 86, 88
Mitsauki Iwago / Minden Pictures: 17, 19, 22-23, 36-37
Photospin: 14, 15 (top), 16 (top), 78, 79 (top), 85 (top)
Ray Maletzki / ISP: 68
Rob Sylvan / ISP: 50
Skip Hunt / ISP: 62 (top)

Cover (clockwise from top left): Mitsauki Iwago / Minden Pictures; Michael and Patricia Fogden / Minden Pictures; Frans Lanting / Minden Pictures; ArtToday; Michael and Patricia Fogden / Minden Pictures

Title spread (clockwise from top left): Mitsauki Iwago / Minden Pictures; Michael and Patricia Fogden / Minden Pictures; Corel; ArtToday; Photospin; ArtToday; Michael and Patricia Fogden / Minden Pictures; Frans Lanting / Minden Pictures

Acknowledgments

With great humility and profound gratitude I offer my thanksgiving before the *Ribono Shel Olam* for all of His kindnesses, and for allowing me the opportunity to open the minds and hearts of Jewish children to the marvels of His creation. May this book be a part of the world's song of praise for Hashem.

"תפארת בנים אבותם" I am dedicating this book to my in-laws, Moshe and Sharon Yanofsky. Their depth of commitment to *Klal Yisrael* is unfathomable. They truly fulfill the maxim of our sages ... "be strong like a lion to fulfill the will of your Father in Heaven ..." We can only stand in the lions' tracks and gape in sheer wonder. They have touched and provided great solace to hundreds even thousands of people. Theirs is a labor of love for Hashem's children, הקב"ה ישלם שכרם.

My parents, Dovid and Tsila Silberstein, as always are a source of strength, inspiration, and infinite love. This book is actually the brainchild of my mother who came up with the idea and coaxed me to write it. Her creativity and good cheer are always evident. May I be זוכה to bask in their sunshine for many more years.

My grandmothers, Mrs. Nechama Roth and Mrs. Bessie Sinensky, are the beloved matriarchs of our family. We love you and hope that you have *nachas* from us.

My children, Avraham Chaim, Rachel, Aharon Shaul, Yecheskel, Sarah Hadas, Aryeh Mordechai, and Shlomo Zalman, always spur me on to greater heights with their *joie de vivre* and endless curiosity. They read and reread the manuscript offering several constructive suggestions, which I incorporated.

Above all, my husband Shimon is my guide, my inspiration, and my partner in my every endeavor. May we merit to see much *Yiddishe nachas* from our family עמו"ש.

This book would not have been possible without the invaluable help of my brother, Yosi Silberstein. A true *talmid chacham,* he researched many of the sources for me from דברי חז"ל. May it be the will of the *Ribono Shel Olam* that he be privileged to do that which gives him most pleasure, delving into the words of our Torah.

A special thank-you to my brother, Eli Silberstein, for giving of his invaluable time.

A very special thank-you to my brother, Chesky Silberstein, for his keen insight when proofreading this book.

To all my special brothers-in-law and sisters-in-law thank you for your friendship and encouragement.

A special thank-you to Rabbi Tzvi Belsky, a noted *talmid chacham* and scholar, for his insight.

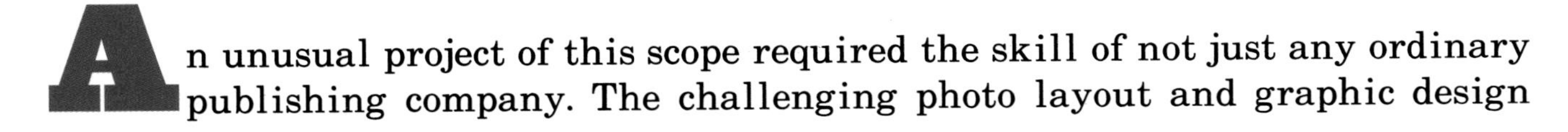

An unusual project of this scope required the skill of not just any ordinary publishing company. The challenging photo layout and graphic design were no simple matters to achieve. This could only be done by a devoted and exceptionally talented staff such as ArtScroll/ Mesorah Publications whose hallmark of excellence is renowned.

The biggest compliment one can pay is to frequent an establishment a second time. There is one fundamental similarity between this book and my first. In both cases I was privileged to associate with the ArtScroll staff who are not only immensely talented, but are special and an absolute pleasure to work with. Truly, they helped make this experience enjoyable. As always, Rabbi Nosson Scherman and Rabbi Meir Zlotowitz provided guidance and focus. Rabbi Menachem Davis read the manuscripts and made some erudite and valuable comments. Rabbi Avrohom Biderman pulled together the many aspects of this complex project.

Thank you, Eli Kroen and Hershy Feuerwerker for your talented efforts in designing this book. Your brilliant creativity is worthy of ArtScroll's standard of excellence. Thank you Chava Esther Ehrlich for helping to coordinate, and Ruchie Reifer for typing.

May ArtScroll continue to succeed in all of its endeavors.

Table of Contents

Introduction

Our souls thrill to the beauty of nature. Mountains, valleys, a sun-soaked orchard, a breathtaking vista — they all stir our senses. Even more compelling than these, however, is probably the animal kingdom, because it has the power of life itself. The sight of zebras and antelopes racing wildly to escape a stalking lion can steal our breath away with its excitement. Children in particular are attracted by the beauty and variety of the animal kingdom. This may be because children are curious; or it may be because they are pure and quicker to see the hand of G-d. Certainly one way to appreciate Hashem's remarkable creation is to study the beauty and complexity of nature.

The *Tanna DeVei Eliyahu* says that a person who wants to appreciate the amazing miracles of Hashem should see the many different types of animals. Are their voices the same? Do they resemble one another? Do they think alike? Do they taste the same? Their many differences are the greatest display of Hashem's greatness. Man casts many coins in one mold, but Hashem creates each creature in a unique fashion. Did you know that there is variety even within one species? For example: each leopard has his own unique spots. There are no two leopards exactly alike in the entire world. This is like human fingerprints; no two are the same.

Many *gedolim,* great Torah scholars, went to zoos in order to see the different types of animals. The *Chida* writes "I myself saw strange, fright-

ening and powerful animals." More recently, the Klausenberger Rebbe related that his great-grandfather, the *Divrei Chaim* of Sanz, visited the zoo in Vienna in order to make the *berachah Meshaneh Habriyos* at the monkey house. When the *tzaddik* was at the lions' den, the lions got up, walked toward him and sat down docilely opposite him. This miraculous story became famous. The Steipler Gaon took his young children to a small zoo in

Camel lies docilely in respect for the respectable.

Ramat Gan, Israel to recite this *berachah* as well. Surely *gedolim* saw Hashem's greatness in the animal world. A spontaneous song of thanksgiving and love for Hashem wells up within us when we behold the splendor of His creation.

Every animal and every part of creation — from the biggest to the smallest — serves Hashem by doing what He created it to do. It is as if each of them praises Hasehm for the way He made it. *Perek Shirah,* which was written by King David and King Shlomo, records the songs of the animals. Every day, every part of creation sings a song of praise before Hashem.

Our Sages tell us that man is the crown of creation. When man sings *Perek Shirah* he empowers the entire creation with the ability to sing before Hashem.

May it be the will of Hashem that this book will open the minds and hearts of Jewish children to the wonders of Hashem's creation. May they burst into songs of love and praise for Hashem, and may their song mingle with the songs of every animal and creature everywhere to be *marbeh k'vod Shamayim* — spread the glory of Heaven.

After Hashem created all of the animals — domestic and wild, fish and birds — He brought them to Adam. Imagine all the millions of different kinds of animals — eagles, doves, hyenas, deer, gazelles, goats, antelopes, bison, orangutans, baboons, chimpanzees, lions, cougars, pumas, cheetahs, bears, coyotes, giraffes, elephants, camels, zebras, donkeys, kangaroos, koalas, mice, skunks, pigeons — all marching in a row before Adam. He looked deeply at each one and with his tremendous wisdom was able to figure out the basic nature of each animal. He then named each accordingly.

Why did Hashem create such a magnificent array of creatures? Our Torah tells us that when man fulfills the will of Hashem, the animal kingdom is there to serve him.

There are many stories in *Tanach* of animals who hastened to do the bidding of *tzaddikim,* righteous people. Did the dove not submit to Noach's will and leave the Ark even though the world outside the Ark looked desolate and destroyed? Do you recall the story of Elisha and the bears who mauled the wicked people who had mocked him? In this book you will encounter stories about elephants, snakes, and lions who lay in submission before the greatness of man. See what heights a person can scale when he fulfills the will of Hashem!

The source material for many of the stories and facts written in this book are the *Midrash, Gemara, Mishnah, Tanach* and their commentaries. They were carefully selected to give the reader an appreciation for the majesty of Hashem's world. So sit back, relax and allow yourself to be transported on a journey to Hashem's wildlife.

אֲרָיוֹת
Lions

אֲרָיוֹת
Lions

A lion roars loudly. His deep voice rolls across the African plain. All the animals listen.

Lions live in large family groups known as "prides." They often roar loudly to keep in touch. They also roar to warn other lions not to trespass on their area. "Stay away! This is our kingdom!"

The lion is called king of the beasts, both for his size and strength, as well as his majestic appearance. Lions are scary. They are meat-eaters with three-inch-long fangs or teeth, razor-sharp claws, and a 400-pound body packed with muscle.

Lions are part of the cat family. The lion is one of the largest cats, slightly smaller than the tiger.

Lions can live in forests and jungles, where there are plenty of hiding places. They prefer, however, to live in wide-open grasslands, where there is plenty of prey: other animals to kill and eat. Lions have ruled wherever they have lived. Other animals fear their ferocious roars. These roars can be heard even five or six miles away. Animals know that lions are unmatched in strength, especially male lions, which are heavier and stronger than the females.

In all of the cat family, lions are the only ones in which it is easy to tell males from females. That's because males have a mane, a thick fur around the neck and face. Usually the female is the hunter. With their slimmer bodies, female lions are more skillful at hunting. In addition, because they have no mane, it is easier for them to stay hidden.

This mane takes four to five years to grow. Hashem created each animal with different features they need to survive. Even the mane is important — it gives the male lion a more threatening look.

A Lion Is Born

It is nearly time for a lioness to give birth. She has carried her cubs for three and a half months. The lioness gives birth to a "litter," a group of babies, every two years, and will have ten to fifteen cubs in her lifetime. She steals away to find a safe hiding place where she will give birth and hide her cubs. She needs a safe spot for the cubs, because she may leave them for hours while hunting. At such times hyenas, leopards, or birds of prey may take the blind, helpless cubs.

Finally, the lioness gives birth. There are four cubs in her litter, which is an average amount. The lion cubs each weigh about three pounds at birth. Their eyes are closed. There are no teeth in their tiny mouths. Their teeth will only start coming out at three weeks. At birth, the cubs do not resemble their mother. While her coat is a golden-honey color, their light brown coats have brownish spots.

These cubs are helpless. While the mother lioness is gone, for as long as forty-eighty hours at a time, the babies stay quiet and still, even if they are very hungry. This is vital to their survival. Animals will kill the cubs if they find them. Hiding is their only defense. It is truly amazing to see how Hashem created an animal with instincts for survival. This means that without anyone teaching the animals, they behave in a certain way to protect themselves.

Over the next few weeks, the cubs nurse from their mother, growing rapidly. They double their weight every week. Imagine if a human baby would do that! All this time, they hide in a secret den with their mother. If the lioness senses danger, she may move them. She carries them in her mouth, holding them by the scruff of their neck.

By the time they are a month old, the cubs can walk well enough to travel with their mother, and she rejoins the pride.

While the young cubs grow, they are learning how to live in a pride with other lions. Much of their day is spent resting and dozing in the sun. Just like house cats on a hot day, they lie on their backs with all four paws outstretched. They are completely relaxed. Sometimes while their mother lies dozing, the cubs frolic in the tall grass. They playfully strike out at each other with their paws. While it is only a game, they are practicing for when they are fully grown and will be hunting on their own.

In the cool of the evening, it is time for the lioness to set off for a hunt with the other lionesses in the pride. She licks her cubs one last time before setting off. In a few weeks, the cubs will be able to join them, but they will not actually be able to hunt until they are at least a year old.

Catching animals is not an easy task. Lions hunt antelopes, zebras, wildebeest, and gazelles, but these animals can easily outrun lions. For this reason, lions are forced to be sneaky. They have to creep in on their prey. This is called "stalking." Hiding until the prey comes close enough to be pounced on is called "ambushing."

A lion's chances of stalking and ambushing are better when it is dark, so lions sleep during the day and hunt at night.

Hashem created a lion with special features for night-time hunting. It can see very well in low light. One reason for this is the large size of its yellow eyes.

The hunt is finally over. The lioness runs back to her cubs, in order to lead them back to the prey. This scene repeats itself until the cubs will be old enough and strong enough to join the hunt.

The first thing the lioness and her cubs eat are the intestines of the prey. The intestines contain many important vitamins and minerals. Hashem created an animal with certain preferences that are important to help him survive.

A new day is dawning. The dry grassland glistens with dew. The sky is getting lighter with every passing moment. Morning sounds are everywhere — the world is slowly awakening.

Mother lioness and her cubs are well fed and content. They sleep through the rest of the day in the shade of an acacia tree.

DID YOU KNOW?

An adult male lion needs 5,600 pounds of meat a year. A male lion might gobble up to 80 pounds of meat in one sitting. In hard times, however, lions might go for days without eating.

Lions can live to be about 25 years old.

Lion Facts

כֻּלָּם בְּחָכְמָה עָשִׂיתָ, *"You created them all with wisdom."*

The lion's scientific name is *Panthera Leo,* which is why people say "Leo the Lion." The tuft on the end of a lion's tail contains a sharp nail. Although scientists and zoologists do not know its purpose, if Hashem created this feature, it surely serves an important function.

Lions are armed with sharp claws on each paw. When not needed, their claws are tucked away into the padded paws, to prevent them from becoming dulled. To sharpen these claws, the lion scratches them on a tree trunk.

Lion Facts

When cubs begin to mature, they start hunting small, slow animals. Such animals are helpless prey. Hashem, therefore, gave them special features for self-protection. A tortoise shell is so tough that even larger animals find it difficult to break through. A whiff of a skunk odor can stop even the most determined lion in its tracks.

When a lion tries to kill a porcupine, the spines can stick the lion's skin. If the wounds get infected, the lion may die. Porcupines are never a first choice for a meal!

Adult lions don't have any natural predators, meaning that there are no animals that hunt lions. Only humans are a threat. During the last hundred years, many lions have been hunted and killed by people for sport.

In addition, as more African and Asian land is farmed or built on, more lions are being pushed out of their natural habitat. They have much less space to roam free. Lions are now on the endangered species list. This means that if we are not careful to give the lions space to roam free, they may be wiped out.

Wonders of Creation

מָה רַבּוּ מַעֲשֶׂיךָ ה׳, *How great are Your works, Hashem!*

A lion's coat helps it blend into its surroundings — a big advantage for hunting. The lion's yellowish color matches the yellowish grass, which is sun dried for most of the year.

- גּוּר אַרְיֵה יְהוּדָה *"Yehudah is a cub and a lion."* In the portion of *Vayechi*, Yaakov blesses his sons before his death. In addition to blessing them, he mentions their special traits. Yaakov likens Yehudah to a lion cub and also to a fully grown lion. He is talking about King David, who comes from Yehudah. While King Shaul was king, David was already a lion cub, as he led the Jews in battle. After Shaul's death, David became the king of Israel. He was then compared to a full-grown lion, king of the beasts.

- Balak, king of Moav, saw how the Jewish nation conquered the mighty Emorites. Balak became very afraid. He hired Bilam, a Midianite prophet, to curse the Jewish nation. Hashem did not allow Bilam to curse His children. Instead Hashem commanded Bilam to bless the Jews. In one of several blessings, he likened the Jewish nation to a lion cub. When a Jew wakes up in the morning, he strengthens himself like a lion to grab *mitzvos*. Immediately, he dons *tzitzis*, recites the *Shema*, and adorns himself with *tefillin*.

  Similarly, just as a lion will not sleep until after he attacks and consumes his prey, so too a Jew does not sleep until he recites the *Shema* and entrusts his soul in Hashem's hands.

A Jew strengthens himself like a lion to catch mitzvos. Immediately, he dons tzitzis, recites the Shema, and adorns himself with tefillin.

The lion has short tufts of hair at the end of his tail. He uses these hairs to flick flies off his body. The lion also uses his tail to erase his tracks. He wipes the ground with his tail until his tracks are gone.

- Although a lion can be very cruel, our sages tell us that he can also be kind. When a lion is hungry he does not immediately prey upon other animals. First the lion sucks on his paw to still his hunger pangs, similar to a human baby. Only when his hunger is overwhelming does he attack other animals.
- For this reason, the Gemara explains that if one sees a person falling into a lion's den, he cannot be a witness and say that he is sure that the person died. Perhaps the lions were not hungry and left him alone. This is different from a snake or scorpion pit, where if a person falls in, he is halachically considered dead. Scorpions and snakes will attack and kill even if they are not hungry. So when Yosef's brothers threw him into a pit filled with scorpions and snakes and he was not harmed, it was a miracle.
- A lion does not usually attack very small animals. Small animals often accompany him when he goes to eat from his prey. They eat the leftovers.

Considering that Noach took such good care of the lion and all the other animals, why did the lion get angry with Noach for being late with one of his meals? It would seem that Noach should have been forgiven this one tardiness. But a lion is king of the beasts and worthy of being served royally. This was especially true of Noach's lions, which were the only lions left in the world!

- The lion fears a holy person. When a lion sees a holy person he moves back.
- The lions surrounding Pharaoh's palace bowed down to Moshe and Aharon.
- Rabbi Shimon ben Chalafta was once walking when he met a roaring, hungry lion. Rabbi Shimon was not afraid for himself; rather, he was concerned that the lion would attack other people, so he prayed. Miraculously, two pieces of meat fell from heaven, one for the lion and one for him. The lion devoured one of the pieces and slunk away. The other piece remained for Rabbi Shimon. It was his reward for being concerned about others.

STORY CORNER

During the days of Rabbi Yehoshua ben Chananya, the Jews petitioned the Roman Caesar for permission to rebuild the *Beis HaMikdash.* All the Jews were gathered together, waiting expectantly for the king's response. The letter arrived. They were very upset when they heard that their request was denied. They then became angry. Some Jews even wanted to rebel against the Roman government. The sages asked Rabbi Yehoshua ben Chananya to speak to the angry mob.

Rabbi Yehoshua told the following story.

After eating from a carcass, a lion once got a bone stuck in his throat. He called out to the other animals, promising a reward to the animal that would succeed in removing the bone. A little bird flew into the lion's mouth and, with its beak, removed the bone. When the bird demanded its reward, the lion said, "It is reward enough that you can tell the other animals that you were in the lion's mouth and emerged unharmed."

Rabbi Yehoshua finished the story and said simply, "It is enough for us that we met the Romans in peace and have emerged unharmed."

STORY CORNER

A man went up with his family to Yerushalayim for one of the *Shalosh Regalim,* the festivals of Pesach, Shavuos, and Succos. In his haste to leave, he forgot to store his bales of wheat in his granary. They were left standing unprotected in the field. The man expected to return and find that the wheat had been stolen or eaten by animals. Upon his return, however, he was pleasantly surprised. Standing guard around the wheat field were none other than a group of lions protecting his wheat. This miracle happened in order to fulfill Hashem's promise, that when the Jews go up to Yerushalayim for the festivals, three times a year, no man shall covet or take their land.

DID YOU KNOW?

Rabbi Chanina ben Dosa once came across a lion. He said, "Oh weak king, did I not make you swear that you would never be seen in *Eretz Yisrael*?" The lion ran off immediately. Suddenly Rabbi Chanina started chasing the lion. He called out, "I apologize for calling you weak. If your Creator described you as strong and powerful, I had no right to say differently. Please forgive me."

If Rabbi Chanina ben Dosa ran after an animal in order to beg forgiveness for insulting it, how very careful we should be never to insult our friends.

POWER OF THE TONGUE

Once upon a time a beloved king became very sick. The king was lying on his deathbed, and no doctor was able to cure his mysterious ailment. Finally, one doctor advised the king to get the milk of a lioness as a possible cure. One daring and loyal servant volunteered. Each day he would cut a slab of meat and throw it before a mother lioness and her baby cubs. Each day he came closer and closer, and the lioness learned to trust him. Finally, one day he managed to get milk from her.

That night the servant had a strange and troubling dream. His limbs and organs were arguing about who deserved the credit for getting the milk. The legs, having brought him to the lioness, said they were the most important. The arms, having taken the milk, felt *they* deserved a pat on the back. The heart boasted of courage and the brain of cunning. Finally, the tongue softly pronounced himself most worthy. The others laughed and mocked the tiny tongue. The tongue decided to show them. The next day the servant brought the milk to the king — and said he had taken it from a dog! The king flew into a rage and ordered the servant's execution. All the organs shook with fear and dread. Finally the tongue bravely spoke up. It explained that the milk was really from a lioness. The king drank the milk and was cured. The servant was then richly rewarded. מָוֶת וְחַיִּים בְּיַד לָשׁוֹן — *Death and life are in the power of the tongue.*

The *Heichal,* or main sanctuary of the *Beis HaMikdash,* was wide in front and narrow in the back, just like the body of a lion. Because of this the *Beis HaMikdash* itself is called אֲרִיאֵ-ל, *Lion of Hashem.*

- "A roaring fire on the Altar"

The *Mizbeiach,* or Altar, of the *Beis HaMikdash,* always had a fire burning. A burning coal had fallen from the heavens in the days of King Solomon and crouched on the Altar like a lion. The flames of the fire resembled the lion's glorious mane during the first *Beis HaMikdash.* During the time of the Second *Beis HaMikdash,* when the Jews were not so righteous, the fire had the form of a dog.

Before they entered *Eretz Yisrael,* the Jews traveled in the desert for forty years. They did so in a very organized fashion. Each tribe had its own flag. The color of the flag was the same as that of the stone of that tribe on the *Choshen,* or Breastplate, of Aharon HaKohen. Yehudah's flag was the color of the heavens. The flag also had a drawing of a lion. This was because Yehudah is compared to a lion.

The tribe of Dan had a stone called *leshem,* which had the color of a lion's eyes. The tribe of Dan is also likened to a lion.

- Yehudah ben Teima says:

Be strong like a leopard, swift as an eagle, run like a deer, and be brave like a lion to do the will of your Father in Heaven.

- The prophet in *Amos* compares Hashem's voice to that of a lion:

אַרְיֵה שָׁאָג מִי לֹא יִירָא, *If a lion roars, who is not afraid?*

Living with the lion is a "night"mare

A lion spends most of the day dozing in the sun. The warmth of the sun diminishes his appetite and makes him sleepy. Only during the cooler evening hours does the lion spring into action, so he remains only a "night"mare. Because of his sensitivity to the sun the lion is not as hungry as other animals of prey. The lion can go several days without eating. Imagine if the lion were to be an active hunter all day long!

An elderly lion was no longer able to hide and conceal himself in order to prey on other animals. He decided to stake out in a cave. Any animal that would venture into the cave would be easy prey. One day a fox came and stood outside the cave. The lion asked the fox why he did not enter. The cunning fox replied. "I see many footprints of animals that entered the cave, but not even one set of footprints going out."

"Incredible ... Fascinating"

When the people of Noach's generation saw that the rain was coming down harder and harder, they realized that they were about to be destroyed. They did not want Noach to live. They tried to grab the *Teivah*, the Ark, and overturn it. Hashem sent lions, who surrounded the *Teivah* for protection.

Why do we compare Hashem's voice to the voice of a lion if Hashem Himself created the lion?

We often compare Hashem to His creations. This is because we cannot even imagine what Hashem's voice sounds like. However, we are familiar with the lion's mighty roar. This gives us just a little bit of an idea of the power of Hashem's voice.

STORY CORNER

King Shlomo built himself a beautiful and marvelous royal throne. It was made of ivory and had six steps leading up to the chair. On the first step stood two golden lions. Facing them were two other golden lions that were hollow. They contained fragrant spices, and as Shlomo would climb the steps, they would release a most pleasing aroma. The throne itself was truly amazing. As King Shlomo would raise his leg, the step would rise and lift him. Music would play. A lion would extend his foot on the right, and an eagle its claw on the left, and King Shlomo would rest on them and climb further.

When Shlomo sat on his throne to judge, witnesses would come before him to testify. As a witness would approach, the throne's mechanism would go into action. Wheels whirred, music played, and lions roared. This would scare the witnesses. They made sure to tell the truth and nothing but the truth.

King Pharaoh of Egypt removed Shlomo's throne from Yerushalayim and brought it with him to Egypt. There he tried to climb up and sit on it. As he took the first step, the lion took a swipe at his thigh and maimed him. Henceforth, he was called the Crippled Pharaoh or Pharaoh N'cho. When wicked King Nevuchadnezzar destroyed Yerushalayim, he set his sights upon conquering Egypt as well. When he came to Egypt he saw this marvelous throne and desired it greatly. He took it with him to Bavel. There he met a similar fate to the hapless Pharaoh. He was bitten by the lion and, in a very unroyal fashion, he fell to the ground.

STORY CORNER

Shoftim

Shimshon was the twelfth *shofet*, or judge of the Jews, during the era of *Shoftim*. He was a *nazir*, a holy person, who was not allowed to drink wine or cut his hair. He had unusual strength. He used his strength to fight the Plishtim, a cruel nation that persecuted the Jews.

Once Shimshon was walking with his parents. They took a shortcut through a vineyard, but Shimshon, being a *nazir*, had to stay away from grapes. He separated from his parents and went around the vineyard. On the way, a lion rushed toward him, ready to kill him.

The spirit of Hashem rested upon Shimshon. He ripped apart the lion with his bare hands, as if it was a young goat. Shimshon understood that Hashem was giving him a sign to encourage him. The Plishtim were not lions. They were just like little goats. They would be easily conquered. After a few days, Shimshon returned to the same spot. The lion's dead body was still on the ground. Bees were swarming around it. The dead lion was serving as a hive for the bees, and honey was on its carcass. Shimshon stooped down, ate some honey, and then continued on his way.

A while later Shimshon married a Plishti woman.

After he married her, he presented a riddle to the young Plishti men who had come to celebrate his marriage. He said, "From the eater came forth food, from the strong one came something sweet." If they could solve the riddle, he would give them a reward.

Shimshon was talking about the lion and honey, but the Plishtim knew nothing about it. They could not figure out the riddle. Finally, they convinced Shimshon's new wife to find out the answer. She got Shimshon to tell her and then she gave the answer to the Plishtim. She was not loyal to Shimshon. A terrible argument between Shimshon and the Plishtim arose because of this.

Shimshon used this opportunity to fight against the Plishtim. He always tried to find reasons to fight the Plishtim, so that they would not harm the Jews.

STORY CORNER

Rabbi Akiva was once traveling. He passed through a town, expecting to be invited to one of the townspeople's homes. No invitation was forthcoming. Rabbi Akiva said to himself, *Whatever Hashem does is for the good.* He decided to spend the night in the field. All he had with him was a chicken, a donkey, and a candle. He lit the candle. Suddenly, a wind blew out the tiny but useful flame. Rabbi Akiva said to himself, *Whatever Hashem does is for the good.* Next, a prowling cat pounced upon his chicken and ate him. Again Rabbi Akiva said, *Everything Hashem does is for the good.* Finally a lion came and killed his donkey. *Everything Hashem does is for the good* was his response.

That night, a regiment of hostile soldiers tore through the town, looting and killing. Had they spotted Rabbi Akiva's tiny flame, or heard his chicken crowing or donkey braying, Rabbi Akiva would probably have been killed by the soldiers. As he said all along, everything Hashem does is for the good.

Not always do we deserve to see this as clearly as Rabbi Akiva did. Nevertheless, we should always remember that everything that Hashem does is for the best.

STORY CORNER

The *Anshei Knesses HaGedolah* consisted of one hundred twenty prophets, elders, scholars, and great rabbis, who were the leaders of the Jewish people during the period between the destruction of the First *Beis HaMikdash* and the beginning of the Second *Beis HaMikdash.* Daniel was a member of the *Anshei Knesses HaGedolah.*

At the time of this story, the king of Bavel was Daryavesh. Daniel was a great favorite of the king. Even though he was Jewish, the king loved Daniel for his wisdom and special character. The other ministers became very jealous. One day they approached Daryavesh with a novel idea. They asked him, "Would you like to establish your kingdom and let everyone know what a great ruler you are?"

Daryavesh, unaware that this was all a plot against Daniel, rose to the challenge. "Of course."

"Well," replied the ministers smugly, "you should make a law that for the next thirty days no one may pray to any

other power besides Your Highness, the king. If any person should dare disobey, he will be thrown into a pit of lions."

Daryavesh agreed.

Daniel, of course, continued to pray to Hashem three times a day.

The wicked and jealous ministers knew that Daniel would continue to pray to Hashem. They planted a young child to spy on him. The child promptly reported that Daniel was praying. The ministers gleefully took the damaging information to the king. Daniel was there also.

King Daryavesh, being very fond of Daniel, refused to believe the ministers. "Bring witnesses!" he declared.

Suddenly, Daniel noticed that the sun was going down. He walked to a private spot and began praying *Minchah.*

The ministers grabbed the opportunity. "Your Majesty," they declared, "is there a need to search for witnesses when Daniel has the audacity to pray right in front of you?"

Daryavesh could say nothing in Daniel's defense. The king simply said, "I forgive him."

The ministers refused to accept this. They declared that it was against the law to pardon such a criminal. They demanded that the king judge Daniel or else give up his kingdom.

King Daryavesh grew fearful of losing the throne. Sorrowfully, he ordered that Daniel be thrown into the lions' den.

The king wanted to cover the pit with a large stone to ensure that none of the ministers would shoot an arrow or throw a stone and kill Daniel. He was hoping that Daniel would be saved. As he threw him in, Daryavesh said, "May the G-d that you always pray to, save you now."

Since Bavel has no quarries, where stones are found, an angel came and brought a stone to cover the pit.

The king prepared a document stating that no one may remove the large stone. The king signed and stamped the document with his signet ring. The ministers were forced to sign as well. In this document, it also mentioned that in the event that Daniel survived, all the signatories would not say that the king had fed the lions before throwing Daniel in. One hundred and twenty ministers signed.

As Daniel was being thrown in, the angel told the lions, "Accept your relative." This was because Daniel came from the tribe of Yehudah, which is likened to a lion. Immediately, the lions jumped one on top of another, circus style, until they reached the opening of the pit and caught him. The ministers left joyfully, but Daryavesh was broken hearted. That night, he refused his sumptuous dinner. He could not eat a morsel of food. He went to bed and tossed restlessly. After a fitful sleep, he awoke. At dawn he ran to the pit and called down quietly. "Was your G-d able to save you? When he saved Chananyah, Mishael, and Azaryah from the burning furnace, it was in the merit of three people. Here you are only one."

Suddenly he heard Daniel. The king stood transfixed as Daniel said, "G-d sent His angels to protect me. Not only was I not bitten by the lions, I was not made uncomfortable in any way. Since an unpleasant odor comes from a lion's mouth, G-d made the lions put their mouths to the ground. This way I would not be uncomfortable." When the king heard Daniel's words he was overjoyed.

As it was very early in the day, His Highness went back to a restful sleep. Later on in the morning, all the ministers came to the palace. Pretending not to know what happened, the king asked. "Should we not go see what happened to Daniel?"

The king stood at the mouth of the pit and called to Daniel. Daniel answered. The king then ordered that Daniel be removed from the pit. Once again the lions jumped on one another until Daniel could climb to the mouth of the deep pit. He was able to safely step out. The ministers stubbornly refused to admit defeat. They insisted that since Daniel would sometimes feed them, the lions recognized him. The king then ordered the ministers to feed the lions. When they were done, the king had the ministers thrown into the lion pit. There were three hundred and sixty lions in this pit and there were one hundred twenty ministers, three lions for each minister. The lions devoured them as soon as they were thrown in, before they even hit the floor!

Killer and Protector

Iddo was a righteous prophet who lived during the reign of the wicked King Yeravam ben Nevat. Hashem sent Iddo to warn Yeravam that he would be punished. Hashem told Iddo not to eat or drink in Yeravam's city, and not to take the same route on his return home. Iddo did not obey Hashem. An old man in the city convinced him to eat and drink in his home. Because Iddo did not do as he was commanded, Hashem decreed that he would not die a natural death. On the way home, a lion killed Iddo. As soon as he died, his sin was forgiven. Hashem protected his dead body. Instead of eating Iddo's body, the lion stood guard, so that no other animal would eat it. Also, the lion left Iddo's donkey alone. This was a great miracle. The donkey crouched at Iddo's feet as if waiting for someone to place the body of the prophet on his back. When his former host, the old man, heard the news, he decided to bury Iddo's body. Imagine the incredible sight that met his eyes! The body was flanked on one side by a ferocious lion, and in the front, by a crouching donkey.

Our Sages tell us that the prophet Chavakuk was miraculously saved after being thrown into a lions' den. Even though the lions were starving they did not harm him. Chavakuk had actually died as a young boy, and the prophet Elisha brought him back to life. Hashem had performed a great miracle for Chavakuk — no wonder the lions would not dare harm him!

STORY CORNER

Lions... and the Holy Land

Whenever the Assyrians would conquer a land, they would exile its people and bring a foreign nation to the conquered land. After the Assyrians exiled the Ten Tribes, their part of *Eretz Yisrael* was destroyed and desolate. The Assyrians brought people called Shomronim, or Kusim, to try to settle in *Eretz Yisrael.* Despite all their efforts, they were not successful. Vicious lions were constantly roaming around and attacking them. It made their lives unbearable.

The Kusim realized that *Eretz Yisrael* is different from any other land. They saw that they must behave a certain way in order to be worthy of living there. They decided to ask the Jews for advice. A *Kohen* told the Kutim that they should convert to Judaism and keep the Torah's commandments. Then they would be able to live peacefully in *Eretz Yisrael.* Because their fear of lions caused them to convert, they are referred to as *geirei arayos*, or "lion-converts."

פִּילִים
Elephants

פִּילִים
Elephants

Mailika is an African elephant. She lives in the forests of Central Africa. A male elephant is called a bull and a female is called a cow. Mailika is a cow.

There are two kinds of elephants, the African elephant and the Asian elephant. The African elephant lives either in the savannah, which are open grasslands, or in the forest. The Asian elephant is at home both in the cool mountain forests of India and in the hot tropical jungles of Southeast Asia. These jungles have a lot of trees and plants crowded together in wet, green places.

How can you tell the difference between an Asian and an African elephant?

A bull elephant can weigh up to 15,000 pounds. Wow! That's about as heavy as a school bus!

The African elephant is larger than the Asian. An African elephant is the world's largest land animal. A bull elephant can weigh up to 15,000 pounds. Wow! That's about as heavy as a school bus! He is about thirteen feet high at his shoulder. That is the height of a tall tractor-trailer. The African elephant has a single bump on the top of his head.

The biggest difference between the African and Asian elephant is the ears. African elephants have huge ears. Sometimes their ears can measure six feet from top to bottom.

The Asian elephant is smaller. A bull will weigh about 12,000 pounds and stand about ten feet tall. Asian elephants have two bumps on the top of their head. And of course, the easiest way to spot an Asian elephant is by its ears. They are quite small.

Like most elephants, Mailika is a gentle and sociable creature. She lives together with her herd. This herd is made up of females and their babies, or calves. The male elephants live in their own herds. The leader of Mailika's herd is her great-grandmother. She is called the matriarch. She is about 65 years old. An elephant may live to be about

70 years old. The matriarch of Mailika's herd, like most elephants, is very intelligent. She really has a good memory. When animals use up the food in an area, they travel or migrate to another spot. The leader remembers many different migration or travel paths. She also remembers where food and water can be found.

It is incredible to see how Hashem equipped each animal with the specialized organs that it needs for survival. An elephant's most important organ is its trunk. An elephant cannot lower its mouth to the ground because its neck is much too short, so Hashem gave it a trunk. The trunk is one of the most amazing organs in the world. It can do everything your hand and arm can do, everything your nose and lips can do — and a few more things besides! Mailika uses her trunk to eat, drink, pick things up, groom, caress, smell, feel, shower, dust, bathe, wrestle, slap, throw, greet, and signal. When the trunk of an elephant gets damaged and can no longer be used, the elephant will die. It cannot eat or do many of the things important to its survival. There are about 100,000 muscles in an elephant trunk, but no bones. This makes the trunk very flexible.

Using these muscles, the trunk can perform powerful actions such as coiling it around a fallen tree and lifting it. But it can also perform delicate, precise actions such as picking a single blade of grass —

מָה רַבּוּ מַעֲשֶׂיךָ ה׳ כֻּלָּם בְּחָכְמָה עָשִׂיתָ! — How great are your creations, Hashem; all of them You created with wisdom!

The trunk is made up of the nose and upper lip. African elephants have longer trunks than their Asian relatives. Their trunks can grow up to eight feet long. African elephants also has two "fingers" at the tip. They use these fingers in the same way we use our forefinger and thumb to pick up smaller objects. The Asian elephant has a shorter trunk with only one "finger" at the tip. An elephant can pick up even a tiny flower with these fingers. It then places the flower in its mouth with its trunk.

The trunk is extremely strong and can uproot a tree and carry heavy loads, even logs weighing up to 600 pounds. But it is also very sensitive to smell and touch. A mother uses her trunk to caress and stroke her baby. Look how Hashem gives "every mother" the tools she needs to care for her children.

Mailika drinks by sucking water into her trunk and then squirting it into her mouth. An adult elephant can suck up to twelve quarts of water into its trunk at one time. It may also squirt the water over its body to cool down.

Indian elephant carrying heavy branches.

DID YOU KNOW?

An elephant's trunk can be used as a snorkel. If an elephant has to cross deep water, it keeps its trunk above the surface so it can breathe even if its whole body is under the water. It is amazing to see how Hashem made animals able to adapt to their environment.

DID YOU KNOW?

With its trunk, an elephant can pick fruit, leaves, and branches from a tree up to a height of twenty feet. That's higher than a giraffe can reach.

Another outstanding feature on Mailika's face are her tusks. Tusks are very long teeth called incisors (in-SIZ-erz) that grow from the upper jaw. These tusks are Mailika's only front teeth. They will grow continuously throughout her life. If Mailika were an Asian elephant she probably would not have tusks. Most Asian females and many Asian males do not have tusks. Some have very short tusks that are not seen outside the jaw. Both male and female African elephants have tusks.

Mailika uses her tusks for many things. They are her tools to dig into the ground when she is looking for water or for digging up roots. Even though elephants are gentle creatures, when provoked they can use their tusks as weapons.

Sad... But True

Elephants are killed by hunters, mostly for their ivory tusks. People pay a great deal of money for jewelry and other items carved from ivory. Years ago, piano keys were made of ivory. To help preserve elephants, most countries have put a ban on ivory trade. This means that buying and selling ivory is forbidden.

Amazing... Unbelievable

The largest single tusk recorded weighed in at 259 pounds. The longest tusk on record measured 11 feet, 6 inches. That's almost twice the size of an average man.

If you look closely at an elephant's tusks, you will notice that one is shorter and worn down more than the other. This is because one is used much more than the other. Just as a person is right-handed or left-handed, elephants are right-tusked or left-tusked. Mailika is a lefty!

"No weight-watchers for Mailika"

Most of Mailika's day is spent eating. She needs a great deal of food to sustain her huge body. She eats about 350 pounds of food a day, mostly leaves and grass. Mailika is an herbivorous animal. This means she eats only plants and fruits, not other animals. She is not carnivorous, which means meat-eating. In the dry season when Mailika cannot find enough leaves and fresh grass, she tears bark from the trees with her sharp tusks and digs up roots.

Mailika spends between sixteen and eighteen hours a day eating. She reaches high into the trees with her trunk to grasp fresh green leaves. She feeds on more than a hundred different kinds of plants. Mailika is also very fond of ripe fruit. Sometimes she even steals fruit and other foods from human campsites. What a naughty elephant!

Although Mailika spends so much time eating, her body cannot break down about half of the food she eats. This portion of food is still undigested when it leaves the body.

Mailika's dung contains many seeds. As she moves around her home range she helps spread plant life. What a marvelous cycle of nature — כֻּלָּם בְּחָכְמָה עָשִׂיתָ — Hashem created the world with such wisdom!

Mailika does not chew the food with her incisors. She has molars: two in her upper jaw, and two in her lower. These molars are toward the back of her mouth. Most elephants go through six sets of teeth. (Humans have two sets: baby teeth and adult teeth.) Mailika is up to her third set. As each set gets worn down it is pushed to the front and then falls out. New sets of molars replace them in the back. The sixth and final set of teeth is very large, the size of bricks. When this set wears out the elephant can no longer eat properly and will soon die. In the wild this usually happens when the animal is about 65 years old. In captivity, for example, a zoo, they can live longer, as they are fed soft food by the zookeepers.

"No soap, radio"

Aside from eating, Mailika's favorite pastime is bathing. Mailika loves water and bathes at least once a day. She often plays with other elephants as she bathes. She and her friends squirt water at each other through their trunks. Also, Mailika lives in Africa where it is often very hot. The water helps cool her body.

Like all elephants, Mailika has thick skin, but it can easily become dry and cracked. To protect her skin from the heat and biting insects, Mailika takes mud baths. She scoops up mud with her trunk and throws it over her back, sides, and head. Sometimes she wallows, or rolls around, in the mud pit. Dust and mud help form a cooling and protective coating on her skin.

Mailika also uses her ears to keep cool. In hot weather, she flaps her ears to create a cooling breeze. This also cools the blood vessels in her ears.

DID YOU KNOW?

Zoologists, the scientists who study animals, can identify individual elephants according to the blood vessel patterns in their ears. This is similar to human fingerprints. No two elephants have the same pattern.

Family members often greet each other by flapping their ears. Imagine the sight of a whole herd of elephants flapping their huge ears wildly. Wow!

Mailika is expecting a baby. She will carry her baby in her body for twenty-two months, almost two years. That is much longer than most animals.

Elephant Baby Facts

- Elephants usually only have one baby at a time. Twins are rare.
- A newborn baby elephant weighs as much as 265 pounds (about the weight of forty average human babies).
- The newborn is helpless at first, but only one hour after its birth the mother gently lifts it to its feet. The baby, called a calf, takes its first unsteady steps.
- A baby elephant sucks its mother's milk with its mouth, not its trunk.
- A baby elephant may suck its trunk for comfort just as a human baby sucks its thumb.

What's in a Name?

An elephant is called a פִּיל (pronounced *peel*) in Lashon Hakodesh, our Holy Tongue. This comes from the word נפל, *to fall,* because a fear *falls* on those that see it, due to its huge size. As a matter of fact, our Sages tell us that the *peel* is like the *nefeelim,* the giants, who lived in *Eretz Yisrael* during the time of the *meraglim,* the spies who Moshe sent to scout out *Eretz Yisrael.* When you look at a *peel* you can begin to imagine what these giants looked like. Also his entire set of teeth "fall out" several times during his life to make room for the next set.

Bare Bones Facts

Despite the fact that an elephant is a big fat animal it is primarily made up of bones! Our Sages tell us that there are two very vulnerable spots on an elephant's body. One of these spots is its massive belly.

After Hashem wrought the great miracle of Chanukah, the Syrian-Greeks continued to attack the Jews from time to time. Lysias, the regent of Syria, organized a vast army of one hundred thousand foot soldiers, twenty thousand cavalry, and many elephants. Just as tanks are used in today's battles, in those days elephants were widely used as the war machine. Each elephant carried a small turret which was like a mini tent, with four soldiers, on its broad back. Each elephant was surrounded by dozens of cavalrymen and hundreds of foot soldiers. In the face of such an army, Yehudah, the Jewish general, was in a difficult position. Elazar, his brother, tried to help. He mistakenly thought that the elephant was carrying the king. Elazer rushed the elephant and drove his sword deeply into the animal's belly. The mortally wounded elephant collapsed, crushing Elazar underneath.

Fascinating Facts

Did you ever see an elephant crouch? Even if you lived in Africa, claiming to see a crouching elephant would raise eyebrows. Only trained elephants crouch, so that acrobats or other animals can jump onto their backs. Generally, elephants don't crouch due to their massive size. They usually sleep or relax while leaning against a tree or some sort of wall.

Story Corner

Our Sages tell us that an elephant is cunning. A group of merchants were once sitting together openly mocking the elephant for its strange and unusual appearance. The elephant ambled over to the riverbank, filled its trunk with water and returned to the merchants. He proceeded to empty the contents of his trunk onto their food. Think twice before you deal with a *"peel."*

A Blessing "In Disguise"

Our Sages tell us that upon seeing an elephant one should recite the blessing מְשַׁנֶּה הַבְּרִיּוֹת, Who makes different kinds of creatures. With this blessing we praise Hashem for creating many different species.

The Gemara says that an elephant is afraid of a mosquito, as it can enter the elephant's trunk, uninvited of course. Although the elephant is massive in size and strength, and the mosquito is a frail little insect, the mosquito can be so irritating that the elephant is literally afraid of it. Hashem created this phenomenon to show that not necessarily does "size" determine strength.

A similar story is told about Titus, the wicked Roman general who destroyed the second *Beis HaMikdash.* and razed much of Yerushalayim. He then traveled home triumphantly to Rome. On his boat were many of the holy vessels plundered from the *Beis HaMikdash.* Titus intended to show them off during his victory parade in Rome. In his mind's eye he saw the cheering crowd chanting Titus — Titus — Titus — ! He threw back his head, puffed up his chest with pride, and caught sight of the heavens. "Ah," he snorted, "G-d of the Jews, I have triumphed over You."

A while later the skies darkened ominously, and menacing clouds appeared. Gale winds began to blow — buffeting the ship to and fro, as huge raindrops pelted down on the hapless crew. Terror gripped the hearts of everyone aboard. They realized that this was Hashem's fury. He was avenging the death of His people and the destruction of the Temple. They were all but lost. Suddenly Titus called, "Bring me to dry land and there we will see who will be victorious!"

The storm stopped. And from the eerie stillness that followed, a Heavenly voice was heard. "Wicked Titus, I have a small and insignificant creature in My world. Mosquito is her name. Go onto dry land and do battle with her."

As soon as Titus stepped foot on Roman soil, a little mosquito entered his nostril. From there it traveled to his brain. It remained there for seven years, knocking, knocking, always knocking. Titus suffered terribly. No doctor was able to help him. At the end, Titus died, a victim of his own arrogance. After his death they opened his brain. Lo and behold, they found a mosquito — the size of a bird.

The Song of the Elephant

The *shirah* or song of the elephant, is מַה גָּדְלוּ מַעֲשֶׂיךָ ה׳ מְאֹד עָמְקוּ מַחְשְׁבֹתֶיךָ, *How great are Your creations, Hashem, how deep are Your thoughts.*

It is very befitting for the elephant to burst forth with such a song of praise for the Almighty. After all, with his tremendous size he bears testimony that the creations of Hashem are so great and mighty.

Follow the Leader

Did you ever see a mighty elephant lumbering along a dirt road, led by a mere lad? Even though the elephant is so powerful, even a youngster can be his master. Our Sages tell us that whoever sees an elephant in a dream will have wondrous things happening to him. This is true, however, only if the man sits astride the elephant in a masterful position. However, if he dreams about an elephant on its own, this is not a good omen, as the elephant is a powerful and potentially dangerous animal.

נְחָשִׁים
Snakes

נְחָשִׁים
Snakes

There are about twenty-five hundred different kinds of snakes in the world. Most people are afraid of snakes. Many people think all snakes are poisonous. In fact, most snakes are harmless; only a few hundred kinds are poisonous. They stay away from people as much as they can. Snakes are among the most interesting creatures on earth.

Snakes are part of the reptile family. Reptiles have scaly skin and are cold blooded.

Snakes live almost everywhere in the world except for very cold places like the Arctic circle, Antarctica, and a few other places. They cannot live in cold places. This is because, like other reptiles such as lizards, turtles, alligators, and crocodiles, snakes

are "cold blooded." This means that the temperature of a snake's body depends upon the temperature around it. Your blood always stays about the same temperature, but a snake's blood changes with the temperature of the air. In the summer, a snake's blood is warm; in winter, its blood becomes cool. A snake will die if it gets too cold or too hot.

When it gets cold, snakes are hard to find. They sleep through the winter in holes and caves. In the spring, thousands of snakes wake up and slither into the sun. Snakes that live in the hot desert creep into holes to hide from the sun.

Snakes can be as short as your finger or as long as a bus. A snake's body contains a heart, lungs, stomach, and other organs. The organs are long and thin, just like the body. A snake has no legs.

DID YOU KNOW?

- A snake never blinks.
- Some snakes can swallow a whole leopard at one time.
- Some snakes can spit poison in their enemies' eyes.

DID YOU KNOW?

That the first serpent, or snake, lived in Gan Eden with Adam and Chava. It was the *Nachash Hakadmoni,* the First Snake. When it was first created, the snake looked very different than it does today. It stood upright and walked on two legs, like a person.

That snake was a very wicked creature. It was brazen, and openly went against the word of Hashem.

The *Nachash Hakadmoni* was also very smart and cunning. He was the king of all the animals. He was so smart, our Sages tell us, that he would have been able to help humans with their business affairs.

Why does the snake look different today?

The snake was more clever and cunning that any other animal. On the day that Adam and Chava were created, he saw them together. He became very jealous. He wanted Chava for himself. But how could he marry her? She was Adam's wife. Finally, he thought of an idea.

He approached Chava and asked, "Is it true that Hashem commanded you not to eat from the trees of the garden?"

This was a trick question. The snake had actually seen Adam and Chava eating from several fruit trees. He wanted to get into a discussion with Chava about the trees. Then he could get her to talk about the "Tree of Knowledge."

Chava responded, "We are allowed to eat from the trees of the garden. It is only from the tree that is in the middle of the garden that we may not eat. Hashem told us that we may not eat from or even touch that tree, or we will die!" Chava was referring to the Tree of Knowledge.

Actually, Chava was adding to Hashem's commandment. Hashem had instructed them only not to *eat* from the tree. They were allowed to touch it.

The snake suddenly pushed Chava against the tree. He said, "Just as you did not die from *touching* the tree, so you will not die if you *eat* from the tree." The sly and wicked snake added, "The reason that Hashem commanded you not to eat from the tree is, because on the day that you do, you will become like Hashem. You will be able to create worlds and will recognize good from evil."

Chava was convinced. She ate from the tree and gave her husband its fruit to eat, as well.

Hashem punished Adam and Chava for not obeying His command. He also punished the snake who had caused Chava to sin. Hashem told the snake, "Because you did this, you will be accursed more than any other animal. From now on you will crawl on your belly. You will eat dust all of your life. I will place a deep hatred between you and the woman. This hatred will exist between her children and your children. This means that people will hate snakes. Man will always try to cut off your head. Since you will have no legs, you will be forced to crawl on the ground and bite man in the heel, and he will crush your head."

Hashem removed the snake's feet forever. He was no longer king of the animals. From then on he would be a lowly slithering creature of the dust.

The hatred that Hashem implanted between the snake and mankind exists forever.

The Sages say that a snake derives no pleasure from biting people. He does so only because he wants to poison and destroy mankind. This increases the hatred between them. Man, too, wants to kill snakes.

Spots

The Midrash relates that the snake's spots are reminders of *tzara'as*, a form of leprosy. Its spots will never heal — even when Mashiach comes. The snake was punished this way because he spoke *lashon hara*, or spoke badly, about Hashem. *Tzara'as* is a punishment for *lashon hara*. Although *tzara'as* is white and snakes have spots of different colors, they still remind us of the sin of *lashon hara*.

DID YOU KNOW?

- Yafes, Noach's son, was in charge of the snakes in the *Teivah*.
- The Sages say that no matter what a snake eats, the food tastes like dust.
- At first one doesn't feel much pain from the poison of a snakebite. The poison travels through the bloodstream until it eventually reaches the brain.

Question Corner

Is it such a terrible curse to eat dust? After all, there is so much dust that the snake never has to worry about food.

Part of the snake's punishment is that his food would be so plentiful that he would never have to pray to Hashem for sustenance. Hashem was so angry with the snake that He never wanted the snake to come to Him for anything. *Bnei Yisrael* are exactly the opposite! We are the beloved children of Hashem. Just as a mother or father are happy when their children speak to them, Hashem loves when we call out to Him in prayer. This is one of the reasons Hashem does not always give us everything immediately. He wants us to come close to Him, and raise our voice in prayer to our Father in heaven.

When Hashem told the snake that he would have to crawl on his belly, the snake responded, "I will be like a fish in water. He too has no feet." At that moment Hashem split the snake's tongue into two parts.

"What A Shame" — I could have used one.

Did you know that if the snake had not sinned, every member of *Klal Yisrael* would have had two trustworthy snakes to serve him? He could have sent one to the north and one to the south to fetch precious stones and pearls for him. He could have used them to tend to his house and garden. Wouldn't that have been nice? "A shame," our Sages say. "What a loss for the Jewish world!"

"Not so bold but very bald"

Once a man who lived in *Eretz Yisrael* had no hair on his head. All his friends and relatives affectionately called him "Baldy" — an undisputably true fact. What happened? He was once on a mountain, peacefully gathering sticks of wood, when he chanced upon a slumbering snake. He was terrified. So intense was his fright that immediately his entire head of hair fell out. His hair never grew back, and, alas, he was called Baldy — forever.

DID YOU KNOW?

The human backbone has about thirty-three small bones called vertebrae. Snakes have many more bones. Some large snakes have as many as five hundred vertebrae! These bones are connected by joints that bend. That is why snakes can easily bend their bodies this way and that, and even twist their bodies into coils. Snakes also have many muscles. They need to be strong in order to push their way along the ground when they move.

Snakes are shiny and sometimes look slimy. Really, they are dry and smooth to touch. A snake's whole body is covered with scales. These scales are hard and tough like fingernails. Hashem created a snake with hard skin so that it can slide easily over the ground.

STORY CORNER

In the days of the holy *Tanna,* Rabbi Chanina ben Dosa, there was a deadly snake called the *arod.* Rabbi Chanina ben Dosa wanted to prove that even though the *arod* was poisonous and dangerous, it was really a person's sins that would cause him to die, and not the snakebite. Rabbi Chanina placed his heel on top of the *arod's* hole. The *arod* bit him. A miracle occurred and Rabbi Chanina remained alive.

Question Corner

How long do snakes live?

Although scientists have rarely observed a wild snake through its life, they can keep track of snakes in zoos. Larger snakes seem to live for twenty to thirty years, and smaller snakes for ten to fifteen years.

How are snakes born?

Some give birth to live babies.

Most snakes lay eggs. The eggs are not hard like chicken eggs. The shells are soft and leathery. A mother snake doesn't usually stay with her eggs. She lays them in a soft warm place, and then slithers away. Depending on the type of snake, the eggs can take from a few days to several weeks to hatch. Once they are laid, the quicker the eggs hatch, the better. Unhatched eggs may be eaten by animals that chance upon them.

A baby snake has an "egg tooth" to help it cut through the shell. The tooth falls off soon after the egg hatches. After they hatch, baby snakes have many enemies waiting to snap them up for a meal. They can be killed and eaten by frogs, pigs, skunks, foxes, birds, and many other animals.

DID YOU KNOW?

Hashem created many snakes with the ability to blend in with the area around them. This helps the snake hide from its enemies.

The beautiful Smooth Green Snake is hard to see because it blends in so well with the surrounding greenery.

Did you know a snake can sense your presence?

Snakes do not see as well as humans, but they can spot even the slightest movement around them. They also have a sense of touch that helps them find their prey and avoid danger. It is amazing how Hashem equips each creature with the apparatus it needs to survive.

Snakes have inner ears, rather than ears outside their bodies. They cannot really hear sounds traveling through the air. Instead, Hashem created them with the kind of hearing sense that they need for survival. They can easily hear ground vibrations — even the quiet rustlings of a little mouse.

Snakes also have an excellent sense of smell. Some, such as the copperhead, have heat sensors in front of their eyes so that they can easily track warm animals.

STORY CORNER

A story is told about a country that was fighting the mighty Roman army. The soldiers of this country came up with a brilliant strategy. While the great Roman ships were coming into the port, the soldiers threw clay jars filled with snakes onto the decks of the ships. The jars smashed. Snakes crawled everywhere. The terrified Romans surrendered immediately.

כִּשְׁמוֹ כֵּן הוּא — As his name so he is

The tail of a rattlesnake has bands of loose skin. These bands rattle loudly when the snake shakes its tail. The rattle is a scary warning. It says, "Bug off!" When the rattlesnake hunts for food, it holds its tail very still.

Interesting Facts

An African Spitting Cobra spots a watching tiger. The tiger is about to attack. Suddenly the cobra spits poison into the tiger's eyes. Its eyes burn and sting terribly, and it slinks off.

Believe it or not:

- It is not hard to outrun a snake. The fastest ones slither at the same speed as you walk.
- The world needs snakes! They are part of the balance of nature. They eat mice and rats that destroy crops.
- If people are bitten, snakes can help! The medicine to treat snakebites is made from their poison.

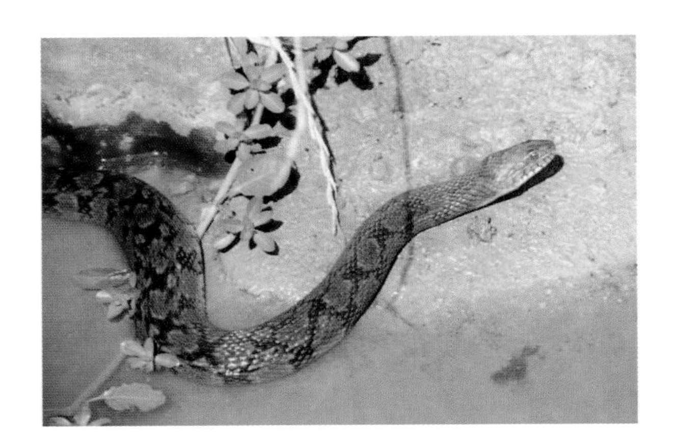

- Snakes can swim.

How do snakes move?

Since Hashem cut off the *Nachash Hakadmoni's* legs, snakes have no legs. They cannot walk or run. Instead, snakes move by curving themselves and then suddenly straightening out or by throwing themselves forward one part at a time.

Snakes can climb trees. They have large scales on their belly that grip the tree. They use their strong muscles to pull themselves up the tree.

DID YOU KNOW?

- Australia is the only continent with more poisonous than nonpoisonous kinds of snakes.
- Two of the most deadly are the death adder and the taipan. The bite of a death adder is often fatal.
- All snakes are meat-eaters. How do they catch and eat their prey?
- Some snakes, such as the garter snake, sneak up on an animal, and then stretch their jaws wide enough to swallow an animal whole. The animal is sometimes larger than the snake's head!
- Some snakes are "constrictors," meaning that they squeeze. They coil around their prey and squeeze until it stops breathing.
- A poisonous snake has hollow teeth called fangs. When a cobra bites an animal, venom flows through its fangs. After the animal dies, the snake swallows it.

Most of the poisonous snakes in the United States belong to a family called vipers.

Make no mistake — poisonous snakes are dangerous and deadly. Poisonous snakes kill more people than lions, tigers, wolves, bears, and sharks all put together.

STORY CORNER

After wandering in the desert for thirty-eight years, the Jews arrived at the boundary of Edom. They hoped to cross Edom and enter *Eretz Yisrael* immediately. The Edomites refused. The weary and disappointed Jews began complaining to Moshe. "Why must we continue to wander in the desert, and live on the *mann,* which is not a natural food?" This was ungrateful of them, since *mann* was a holy gift from Hashem and they had eaten it all those years in the desert.

Hashem said, "Let the snake to whom all things taste like dirt punish those who were given the *mann,* which has every flavor they want."

As a punishment for complaining about the *mann,* Hashem sent poisonous snakes. Many Jews were bitten and died.

The people realized that they had done wrong. Falling down before Moshe, they begged him to pray for them. He did of course and Hashem instructed him to make an image of a large venomous snake and hold it high up. Everyone who was bitten should look at it and would remain alive. Moshe made a copper snake and placed it on a high pole. Everyone who gazed at it was saved.

Of course, it was not the snake itself that dispensed life or death. By raising their eyes to the heavens and seeing the image of the very same creature that had bitten them, they realized that the snake does not kill; rather, the *aveirah* does.

Shlomo Hamelech, the wisest of men, taught us in *Sefer Mishlei* that when Hashem is pleased with the ways of man, even his enemies make peace with him.

Rabbi Elazar, the son of Rabbi Shimon bar Yochai, was once traveling through a desert with his friends. The illustrious group came upon a lush oasis, and sat down to learn Torah. As they were sitting, a huge snake approached. To the utter astonishment of his friends, Rabbi Elazar addressed the snake. "Snake, turn back, for the man whom you were sent to kill has repented." The serpent stopped in its tracks, but after a few minutes, came back. Rabbi Elazar once again demanded that the snake retrace its steps.

"Go back to your cave. A wicked heathen is resting there, planning to kill a certain Jew. Go and kill him." The snake promptly reversed its direction. Rabbi Elazar turned to his wonderstruck friends and explained: "This snake was on its way to kill a sinful Jew, but he had already repented his sin. When I first ordered the snake to retreat, it refused to do so. Once a snake is sent to kill a human being, it will not retreat until it fulfills its mission or unless another person is substituted. A snake will refuse to come back emptyhanded."

The group left the oasis and came to the cave where they found the dead heathen. That very same snake was now coiled around his body in a viselike death grip. "Blessed is Hashem Who carries out his purposes through different kinds of creatures!" exclaimed Rabbi Elazar. He then examined the dead man's pockets and removed a purse full of gold dinars. The sages then returned to the oasis. There they met a brokenhearted Jew. He told them that his purse, which he was going to use to support a poor bride, was stolen by a wicked heathen.

Rabbi Elazar took the Jew by the hand and led him to the cave. Upon seeing the dead heathen, the Jew rejoiced and praised Hashem. Rabbi Elazar returned the purse and then approached the dead body. "Snake, snake," he said. "You have done well. Now return to your hole, for I decree that never again will you harm any human being." The snake uncoiled itself from the heathen's body and returned to its lair.

STORY CORNER

Shmuel Hanavi anointed Shaul to be the first king of the Jews. Not all the tribes of Israel accepted Shaul. Some of the people of Yavesh Gilad, in the territory of Menashe, were among those that spoke *lashon hara,* slander, about Shaul. They felt he was unworthy to rule the entire Jewish nation. As a punishment for speaking against the new king, Hashem sent Nachash, king of Ammon, who threatened to attack and destroy the town of Yavesh Gilad. Nachash means snake, and indeed King Nachash was as evil and dangerous as a snake. Our Sages tell us that one who speaks ill of others deserves to be punished by snakes. From the time that the snake in Gan Eden enticed Chava to eat from the Tree of Knowledge with his evil tongue, the snake has become a symbol of speech that is used for evil.

The people of Yavesh Gilad were terrified. They sent a message to Nachash stating that they were ready and willing to make a peace treaty with him and to serve him.

Nachash arrogantly agreed on one condition. He would only make peace with them if each member of Yavesh Gilad would be blinded in his right eye.

When Shaul heard the terrible news, Hashem's spirit suddenly came upon him. He quickly managed to gather together three hundred and thirty

thousand soldiers. He divided his camp into three groups. At dawn Shaul staged a surprise attack on Ammon and defeated them. Many died. The "snake," Nachash HaAmmoni, had to slither away in disgrace. Shaul was then unanimously accepted as the new king.

A few years later Shaul was killed by the Plishtim in battle. They beheaded him and stuck his head on a pole in the temple of their main idol, Dagon. His body and the bodies of his sons were hung up on a wall. When the people of Yavesh Gilad heard what happened, they decided to go and rescue Shaul's body. They wanted to repay him for saving them from wicked Nachash. They risked their lives and brought the bodies of Shaul and his sons back to their land, where they buried them under an oak tree.

STORY CORNER

Shulamis, daughter of the famous sage Rabbi Akiva, was getting married. On the day of her wedding, servants scurried to and fro with heaping trays of food and delicacies. They were busy preparing for the wedding feast of this very important family. No one noticed the very hungry beggar standing by the door. No one that is, except for the bride herself. Shulamis courteously invited the beggar in and seated him comfortably. She brought him heaping plates of hot food, personally serving him until he ate his fill. Shulamis did all this quietly. She did not even tell her parents.

Before the wedding ceremony, Shulamis took a stroll in the garden. After a while she stopped to rest. Sitting next to the garden wall, she pulled out the gold pin that held her hair together. She stuck the pin into the wall, closed her eyes and nodded off to sleep. She awoke a while later, refreshed and invigorated. She was thinking about the wedding and forgot about the pin.

The next day, Shulamis was walking in the garden with her parents, Rabbi Akiva and Rachel. As they were strolling along, Shulamis spied her gold pin, embedded in the garden wall. With a cry of delight she removed the pin from the wall. Her pleasure at recovering her beautiful pin quickly turned to horror as she beheld a dead snake dangling from the end of the pin. The snake had obviously been killed by the sharp edge of the pin.

White-faced, she glanced at her equally aghast parents. Rabbi Akiva then recalled that many years ago, when Shulamis was a child, a group of stargazers had warned him that Shulamis would die on her wedding day.

Rabbi Akiva asked Shulamis if she had done anything special on the day of her wedding. Shulamis thought and thought and finally remembered how she took care of the hungry beggar. "My daughter," said Rabbi Akiva. "Charity saves from death. In the merit of feeding that poor beggar your life was spared."

Dear reader, the next time an opportunity arises to perform an act of kindness for an unfortunate person, or to give charity to the needy, remember that in this merit, Hashem will bless you and protect you from harm.

Snakes grow quickly, but their skin doesn't stretch. When the skin gets too tight, the snake has to shed it. This is called "molting." The snake rubs its head on something rough, like a log. After a few minutes, the skin begins to peel. The snake slides forward and right out of its skin! Underneath is a new, bright and shiny skin. It keeps on growing. Soon it will be time to molt again. Young, quickly growing snakes may molt six or more times a year. Unlike people, snakes never stop growing.

DID YOU KNOW?

When a snake is ready to molt, its eyes turn milky white. The snake is almost blind for a week, so it stays hidden.

Molted Snakeskins

The Song of the snake as recorded in *Perek Shirah* is סוֹמֵךְ ה׳ לְכָל הַנֹּפְלִים וְזוֹקֵף לְכָל הַכְּפוּפִים, *Hashem supports all of those who have fallen, and He straightens all of those who are bent.* The snake who cannot stand is surely in a position to praise Hashem for supporting the fallen and the bent. If Hashem provides for the snake, who has fallen so low, surely he also takes care of His beloved children even when they have sinned and fallen.

Dear reader,

In this book, we have seen a very small part of Hashem's beautiful world.

I hope it gave you a glimpse of the majesty of His animal kingdom and how He provides what His creations need. Surely, when we look at Hashem's world we will recognize His greatness and increase our love for Him.

I pray that this book will bring about an increase in the honor of Heaven and the love for Hashem.

This volume is part of
THE ARTSCROLL SERIES®
an ongoing project of
translations, commentaries and expositions
on Scripture, Mishnah, Talmud, Halachah,
liturgy, history, the classic Rabbinic writings,
biographies and thought.

For a brochure of current publications
visit your local Hebrew bookseller
or contact the publisher:

Mesorah Publications, ltd

4401 Second Avenue
Brooklyn, New York 11232
(718) 921-9000